Maria,

Wishing

more of

Have a great holiday

full of happy days.

Best wishes

Edith

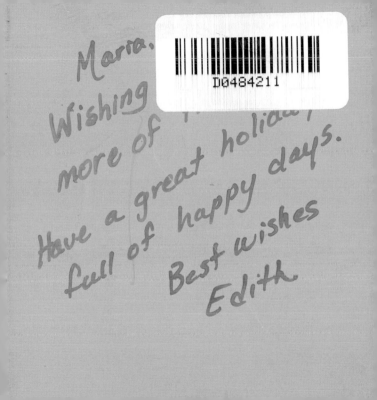

OTHER GIFTBOOKS IN THIS SERIES

hope! dream!   *love*
friend   *smile*

Printed simultaneously in 2003 by Exley Publications Ltd
in Great Britain and Exley Publications LLC in the USA.

12 11 10 9 8 7 6 5

Illustrations © Joanna Kidney 2003
Copyright © Helen Exley 2003
The moral right of the author has been asserted.

ISBN 1-86187-560-6

Written by Pam Brown
Edited by Helen Exley
Pictures by Joanna Kidney

Printed in China

Exley Publications Ltd, 16 Chalk Hill, Watford, Herts WD19 4BG, UK
Exley Publications LLC, 185 Main Street, Spencer MA 01562, USA.
www.helenexleygiftbooks.com

A HELEN EXLEY GIFTBOOK

happy day!

BY PAM BROWN
PICTURES BY JOANNA KIDNEY

Good luck always.
May the doors you knock on
open to you
– and reveal the unexpected
and the wonderful.

MAY THIS BE ONE OF THE DAYS...

...when the mind discovers
undreamed-of things.
...when the eye is suddenly astounded.
...when the ear is overwhelmed by glory.
...may this be one of the days
of new beginning
when we seem to see
to the very edges of the universe.

We are a part of all that is.
The branching trees find echoes
in our veins.
The spring that calls
the buds to break
and the swallows to return
– waken us to joy.
May you, today
and always,
share the wonder
of the world.

May your life have diamond days.

I wish you waking to sunlight
shining through closed curtains,
birdsong,
hot showers,
fresh bread,
work that you long to do.

*I wish you things
to catch your heart in beauty, in joy
and in amazement.
Things
that will make you shout with laughter
and stir you to excitement.*

May you find the little paths
bright with birdsong,
hedged with flowers,
that others never see.

May you know
contentment,
delight,
and your fair share of absolute joy.

May the road lead
through a sunlit countryside.
May no river be too deep to wade,
no rock be too difficult to climb.

May you travel to wonderful places,
See wonderful things,
Meet wonderful people.
May you discover things
you'd never dreamed of.

May every road you take

May you always choose the path
that leads to the greatest happiness.

be easy for your feet.

May you,
today and always,
   share the wonder of the world.

– the swallow's rust-feathered throat,
   – the delicate hands of a mouse,
– the jewel-like eyes of a toad,
   – mist across meadows,
   – black star-spattered skies, lark song,
         country silences, clear seas
   and shimmering sands.

I wish you
the beauty of silence,
the glory of sunlight,
the mystery of darkness,
the force of flame,
the power of water,
the sweetness of air,
the quiet strength of earth,
the love that lies
at the very root
of things.

I wish you... growth and form and scent,
Leaf and bud and flower,
Discovered or nurtured,
Brief, precious,
Unique.
Life returning after winter.

✫

I wish you quiet sleep,
dreams of meadows, deep
in flowers and grass,
of oceans calm and flecked with silver,
of islands
hushed by gentle waves,
of countries of your own invention,
of easy talk with friends,
of roads leading to a reunion,
of sorrow comforted,
of hope restored.

May you find
happiness in a quiet,
perpetual rejoicing
in small events.

MAY YOU KNOW
SHINING DAYS —
DAYS THAT WILL BRIGHTEN
ALL THE DULL ONES
THAT LIE BETWEEN.

Happy Day!

A most ordinary morning.

A most ordinary street.

The cold of autumn.

And yet,

each privet hedge

is strung with pearls of light.

The world's aglitter in the rising sun.

And all is yours.

HOW SMALL THE BOAT
                IN WHICH EACH LIFE SETS SAIL,
HOW GREAT THE OCEANS
                        AND THE DANGERS.
        MAY THE SUNLIGHT TOUCH
                    THE WAVE TOPS
THAT SHIFT AND SHIMMER.
            MAY CLEAN WIND TAKE THE SAILS.

May there always, always
  be something you want to learn,
somewhere
    you want to go,
something you want to do,
    someone you want to meet.

May you always
have room in your life
for another friend.

May there always be friends
to share your laughter,
your troubles
and your victories.

I wish you the joy of always
having someone
to share things with.

I WISH YOU THE JOY OF
THE RIGHT ONE
REALIZING
JUST WHO YOU REALLY ARE INSIDE
— AND LOVING YOU FOR IT.

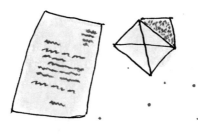

I wish you letters:
in handwriting that you recognize
at once; in handwriting
that you have not seen for years;
in handwriting totally unknown.
I wish you letters full of praise,
full of encouragement;
letters of thanks and love.
I wish you letters of apology
from manufacturers
– with unexpected prizes.

I wish you the joy of... ✳

Spotting your missing cat

plodding up the path.

Seeing your luggage come safely round the carousel.

Opening a letter from someone

whose address you have lost.

Seeing someone's face light up at the sight of you.

Finding the perfect gift.

Taking off your smart shoes.

Seeing the one you love at the end of the platform.

Pistachio nuts.

Renoir. Walking in the rain.

I wish you the happiness
of always having something to give;
– a surprise, affection,
– freshly-baked scones,
paperbacks, seedlings and apples,
– a hand with the tidying up,
a fetching-in of shopping, a feeding of cats,
a listening ear
– comfort – time.

May all your kindnesses be remembered
and all your faults forgiven.

I wish you quiet times
of hope and recollection.
And sleep
as gentle as a stream.

I WISH YOU THE JOY OF ROADS –
roads over the high moors,
tree-lined country lanes,
deep, lost greenway tracks,
harebells and hidden spring, curlew cry,
larks lifting in the clear, bright air.
Roads bucketing down hillsides to the sea,
the road to Rome, the road to the sea,
the road to the Isles.
...the road home.

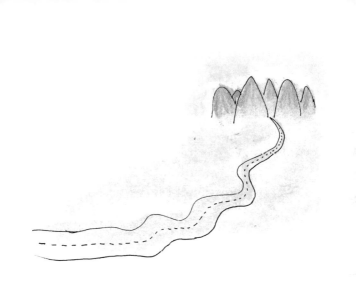

Have fun.
Enjoy the year that lies ahead.
Open your arms
to all the delight –
of flowers and music,
every lovely thing.
Of adventure and astonishment.
Of love.
Of friends you've yet to meet.
Be brave.
Be curious. Be courteous.
Discover a wider world.

I hope for you
the discovery
  of what you are really good at
and what you really want to do.
  And that you'll have the courage
    and the luck
  that makes your dreams come true.

How can I wish you anything?
Save that you find
what you want to do and do it.
Well.

I wish you the joy
of mastery –
of your own muscles,
of a boat, of a bike, of a horse,
of paint and canvas,
plain and purl, pastry, engines,
calculus or French.
Anything. Everything.

I wish you the joy of "I see!
I understand!"

I wish you the happiness
of taking your shoes off
after a hard day's shopping.
– the happiness of an elaborate
scratch on waking.
– a resounding sneeze.
– stretching till you crack.
– a yawn that goes on
and on and on.

May you never feel lost...

Growing more despondent
with every passing minute
        – and then to see
the looked-for figure.
        The surge of joy.
The leaping of the heart.
The slowing down of time.

May you hold
...calm
when the world
is full of sound and fury,
...love
when the world
seems cruel and heartless.

There will be times
when much will be asked of you.
I wish you the courage
and endurance
and the wisdom you need.

*May you always
find exactly the right words
to put bullies in their place.
May you always find the courage
to stand against evil.*

May every hardship
        give you greater strength.

    May great happiness be yours
– but if some darkness comes,
            may you always find
                a hand to guide
        and comfort you,
            a voice to cheer you.

I wish you the happiness
   of finding exactly the right words
...for those in distress
...for those rejoicing in good fortune
...for those afraid or uncertain
   ...for those you love.

May something you do or say
make all the difference
         to someone's life.

Here is a gift.

A night of gentle rain.

The scent of grass.

A pattering against the window pane.

A sighing

of soft air shifting

the spangled leaves.

A time to share in silence.

May you find quietness
at the very heart of your life
that would remain tranquil
and certain
whatever befell.

There are times
when the heart and mind
are overwhelmed by silence.
Times when the roaring world
retreats
and leaves us to discover peace.
So brief a respite.
Cherish the moment.

I wish you
old loves,
old friends
and old contentments.

MAY YOU KNOW
THE JOY OF FREEDOM
— AND THE JOY OF HAVING ROOTS.

To walk in sunlight
along a lonely beach.
To sprawl in meadow grass.
To swim in the transparency of water.
To come home to those you love.

I wish you

    the happiness of love,

that does not change with change

    that shines

    as surely in age as in youth.

May you always
be a child in curiosity,
delight and eagerness.

May the winds be fair
        and the currents kind.
May the charts be true,
the channel clear, the landfall certain,
        the holding good
    – and at the end,
            a safe haven.

I WISH YOU ALL GOOD THINGS
BUT MOST OF ALL
I WISH YOU COURAGE.
WHATEVER HAPPENS,
BELIEVE IN YOURSELF
AND GO ON.

MAY YOU GROW OLD HAPPILY —
UNTIL YOU CAN
NO LONGER COUNT THE CANDLES
ON YOUR BIRTHDAY CAKE.

I wish you joy
and peace
and deep contentment.
And always,
always,
love.

Helen Exley runs her own publishing company which sells giftbooks in more than seventy countries. She had always wanted to do a little book on smiles, and has been collecting the quotations for many years, but always felt that the available illustrations just weren't quite right. Then Helen fell in love with Joanna Kidney's happy, bright pictures and knew immediately they had the feel she was looking for. She asked Joanna to work on *smile*, and then to go on to contribute the art for four more books: *friend*, *happy day!*, *love* and *hope! dream!*

Joanna Kidney lives in County Wicklow in Ireland. She juggles her time between working on various illustration projects and producing her own art for shows and exhibitions. Her whole range of greeting cards *Joanna's Pearlies* – some of which appear in this book – won the prestigious 2001 Henries oscar for 'best fun or graphic range'.

Acknowledgements: PAM BROWN, CHARLOTTE GRAY, PETER GRAY: published with permission © Helen Exley 2003.